Match Mine
Language Builder

Concept and Development
Miguel Kagan

illustrations
Erin Kant

Publisher
Kagan Publishing

Kagan

Kagan Publishing
981 Calle Amanecer
San Clemente, CA 92673
1 (800) 933-2667
www.KaganOnline.com

ISBN: 978-1-879097-21-6

Table of Contents

30 Match Mine Games!

How to Play

Match Mine

Partners, on opposite sides of a barrier, must communicate with precision in order for the Receiver to match the Sender's arrangement of game pieces on a game board.

Sender

Receiver

Students pair up. Partners sit on opposite sides of a barrier so they can't see each other's game board. They each have an identical game board and identical game pieces. One student is the "Sender" and the other is the "Receiver." To start, the Sender first lays out all of his/her game pieces on the game board in any arrangement without talking to the Receiver. The Sender cannot move the game pieces once they are all set in place. The object of the game is for the Sender and Receiver to communicate clearly so the Receiver can perfectly match the Sender's arrangement. To make a match, the Sender describes his/her arrangement by explaining the location of each game piece. The Receiver listens carefully and follows the Sender's directions. On the following pages, you will find detailed instructions, plus game variations.

Match Mine: Language Builder
Kagan Publishing • 1 (800) 933-2667 • www.KaganOnline.com

Getting Ready

Partners, one the Sender, the other the Receiver, sit on opposite sides of a barrier with identical game boards and game pieces.

1. Sender Creates Arrangement

The Sender arranges his/her game pieces on his/her game board while the Receiver waits quietly. For the Barnyard Animals game, the Sender places his/her animals in the barn.

2. Sender Directs Receiver

The Sender gives the Receiver directions to match the Sender's arrangement of game pieces on the game board. Instructions may sound like: "The horse is in the top window of the barn. Below the horse on the right is the turkey…"

3. Partners Check

When finished, partners carefully set their game boards side by side to check for accuracy. "OK, it sounds like we have a match, let's check."

4. Praise and Plan

The Receiver praises the Sender for his/her instructions and they develop improvement strategies. "Great job describing your barnyard layout. Next time, let's call the female chicken a hen."

5. Switch Roles

The Receiver now becomes the Sender and the Sender becomes the Receiver. The pair plays again.

Match Mine

introduction

Why Play Match Mine?

The games in this book are specifically designed to build language skills and vocabulary. They are ideal for students learning English as a second language, for students learning a foreign language, and for little ones developing their native language skills. In addition, Match Mine is a fun format yielding many important learning benefits for students:

• Develops academic vocabulary
• Improves verbal communication
• Enhances ability to give directions
• Promotes active listening
• Nurtures cooperative skills
• Promotes role-taking ability
• Develops visual analysis
• Increases spatial vocabulary (right, left, top, etc.)

Ways to Play

• Whole Class Activity
The whole class can play Match Mine at the same time. Each pair receives a Match Mine game set.

• Learning Center
Match Mine can be done at a center. At a center, you may have two of the same games set up to accommodate four students. At another center, there may be different games.

• Sponge Activity
Match Mine is a great activity students can play when they've finished their work.

What's in this Book?

Intro Page

For each of the 30 games in this book, you will find an introduction page that shows the game board, game pieces, and lists the vocabulary that game develops.

Game Board

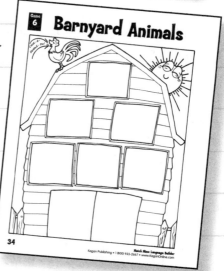

Each of the 30 games have one unique game board. The game board is a reproducible page. Make one copy of the game board for each student playing (2 game boards per pair).

Game Pieces

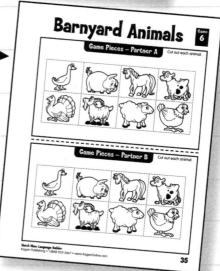

There is an identical set of game pieces for Partner A and Partner B. If they fit, the game pieces for both partners are on the same page. Otherwise, the game pieces are on two pages, one set per page. Make a copy of the game pieces so each student receives an identical set. Students cut out each game piece.

Playing Tips

Sponge Activity

Pairs will finish at different rates. When they're done let them play a different Match Mine game or play the same game using a variation described on the following pages.

Creating a Barrier

A barrier is set up between each pair. The preferred barrier is a file folder barrier. To make a file folder barrier, you will need two file folders and a paper clip. Place the file folders back to back and paper clip the top of the file folders together as illustrated. Next, open the file folders and spread out the bases so the barrier is self-standing. Instead of a paper clip, you can use staples or tape to keep the file folders together, but the paperclip doubles for a storage closure as described on page 12.

Color Card Stock Paper

Copy the game board and game pieces on different color paper. Card stock is preferable if available because it makes the game more durable for re-use. Having a different color game board and game pieces makes the game pieces easier to see.

Laminate Games

For extra durability, laminate the game board and game pieces. Laminate the game pieces before they are cut out.

Alternative Barriers

Any barrier will work as long as students can hear each other, but can't see each other's game board or game pieces. Alternate barrier options include:
• Large book
• Binder
• Students sit back to back

Model it

To introduce Match Mine to the class, model it using either an overhead projector or role play it.

Overhead Method: Provide each student with a game board and game pieces. Copy the game board onto a sheet of transparency film and copy the game pieces onto another sheet (preferably colored film).

With the projector turned off, first arrange your game pieces on your game board and then give directions to the class. Each student builds his or her own game board. When it is time to

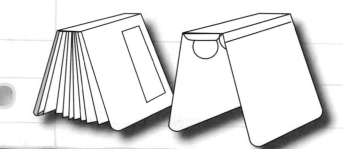

check how well the students have matched your arrangement, turn on the overhead projector.

Role-Play Method: You role play with another student. The student is the Sender and you are the Receiver. Play dumb, purposefully misinterpreting vague directions. An example: If the student says, "Place the circle on top of the square," you place the circle directly over the square, covering it up! The student meant above the square. If there is any ambiguity in the student's instructions, intentionally "go wrong" in order to demonstrate the importance of precise directions.

Playing to Learn
Students can come up with strategies to successfully make a match without developing their language and vocabulary skills. For example, they can say I organized the pieces from biggest to smallest. Although this is quite clever, the real intent of the game is to use the target vocabulary. Tell students that the true goal is to build language skills, so they should try to be as descriptive as possible.

Do the Walkabout
As students play in pairs, walk around and eavesdrop in. This is a great time to make corrections and if you notice similar problems, to stop the class and make an adjustment.

Checking for Accuracy
When students think they made a match, they check for accuracy. The best way to check is for the Receiver to carefully move his/her game board side by side with the Sender's game board. Then, they check each game piece and pat each other on the back or do some celebration for each correct piece. If they are not side by side and do not check each piece, they may think they have made a match when in actuality they haven't.

Processing Errors
If students find a error, they discuss why they made an error. Was the wrong vocabulary used? Was a direction not followed or interpreted correctly? Students find where they made a mistake and discuss how they can communicate more clearly next time.

Match Mine

Variations

peek at the answers on the back. Students use the written description to try to make a match. When they think they have it correct, they flip over the instructions and compare their arrangement with the answer.

Single Sender

Match Mine can be played as a whole class with a single Sender. The Sender can be the teacher or one student. The rest of the class are the Receivers. The Sender (at the overhead) builds an arrangement, and describes it to the whole class. The Receivers follow the Sender's instructions. Because the whole class format cuts down on active participation, it is suggested only for younger students or for initial demonstrations.

Pass-A-Note

Students write directions, passing notes back and forth, communicating only in writing.

Arrange-What-i-Write

Every student gets an extra game board, so they each have two game boards and one set of game pieces. They each arrange their game pieces on one game board. On the second game board, they make a note of the location of each game piece. Then, they each describe their arrangement as fully as possible in writing on back of the game board (no drawing allowed). Students then switch instructions. Tell them they are not allowed to

Teams of Four

Match Mine may also be played in teams. Each team is provided two sets of game pieces, two game boards, and one barrier. Pairs are seated on each side of the barrier with their game board and game pieces. One pair is designated as Senders, the other as Receivers. For equal participation, the two Senders alternate giving instructions. Receivers discuss placing the game pieces and alternate placing them.

Silent Partner

To add a degree of difficulty, introduce a fun variation called "Silent Partner." In this variation, only the Sender is allowed to speak. The Receiver cannot ask for clarification during the game. This requires very precise instructions and active listening.

Taking Turns

Instead of the Sender building a design and the Receiver matching the design, partners take turns placing each piece. They alternate roles of Sender and Receiver after placing each game piece.

Yes or No

Yes or No borrows from the game 20 Questions. The Sender builds an arrangement. When done, the Receiver tries to match the layout but, like 20 Questions may only ask the Sender "Yes" or "No" questions.

Is the dragonfly above the caterpillar?

Is the wasp next to the butterfly?

Is the butterfly on the right side?

Is the ladybug in the center?

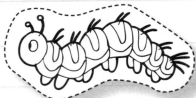

Is the caterpillar on the left side of the wasp?

Storage Tips

We recommend using file folders as barriers because they fold flat, ideal for storage. When students are done playing, have them place their game pieces in separate envelopes or resealable sandwich baggies. Then, they fold the barriers closed with the game boards and game pieces baggies inside and use the paper clip to hold it all together. Store the class set together. If you store your Match Mine games this way, it makes it quick and easy to pass out the games and set them up again for next use.

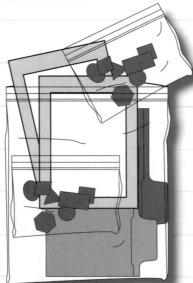

Put Away Each Game Separately

- Place game pieces into 2 separate sandwich baggies or envelopes
- Fold game boards into file folders
- Paper clip the set together
- Insert the entire set into a large resealable bag or catalog envelope

Match Mine Shapes

Store Games Together
Keep all the same games together and label the class set so they are ready for next time!

A Feast of Food

Partner A places food game pieces on the table and plates game board. Partner B cooperates with Partner A to make a match.

Game Board

Game Pieces

Vocabulary

- Chicken
- Hamburger
- Hot dog
- Meatballs
- Pasta
- Pizza
- Plate
- Salad
- Sandwich
- Spaghetti
- Steak
- Table
- Tacos
- Turkey

A Feast of Food

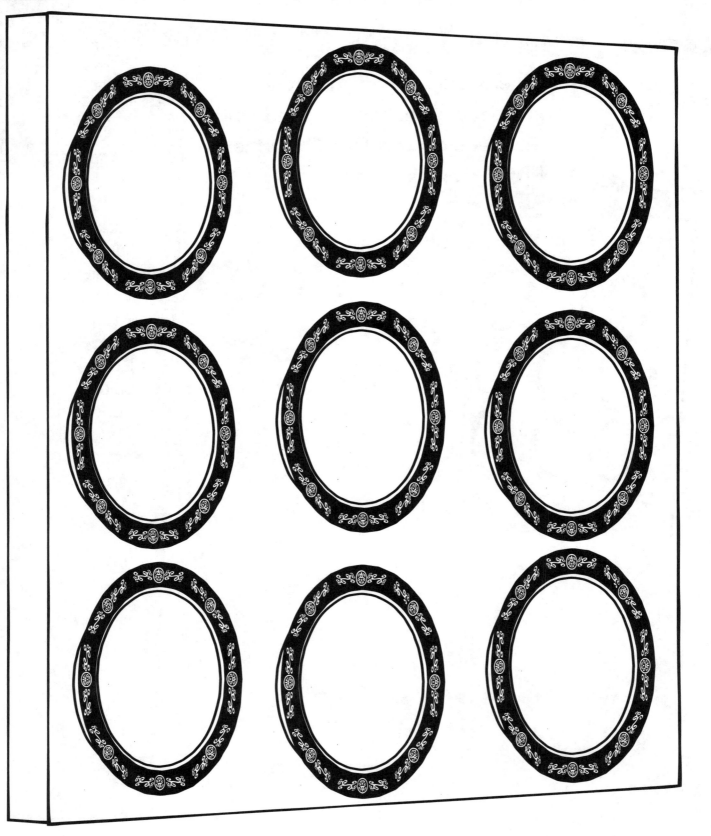

Match Mine: Language Builder
Kagan Publishing • 1 (800) 933-2667 • www.KaganOnline.com

A Feast of Food

Game Pieces – Partner A   Cut out each item.

A Feast of Food

Game Pieces – Partner B   Cut out each item.

Match Mine: Language Builder
Kagan Publishing • 1 (800) 933-2667 • www.KaganOnline.com

Partner A places air transportation game pieces on a cloudy sky game board. Partner B cooperates with Partner A to make a match.

Game Board

Game Pieces

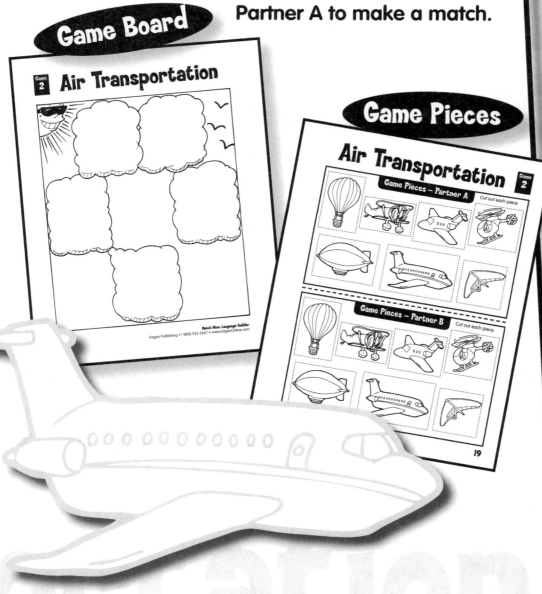

Vocabulary

- Airplane
- Bi-plane
- Birds
- Blimp
- Cloud
- Hang glider
- Helicopter
- Hot air balloon
- Jet
- Sky
- Space shuttle
- Sun
- Zeppelin

Air Transportation

Match Mine: Language Builder
Kagan Publishing • 1 (800) 933-2667 • www.KaganOnline.com

Air Transportation

Game Pieces – Partner A

Cut out each piece.

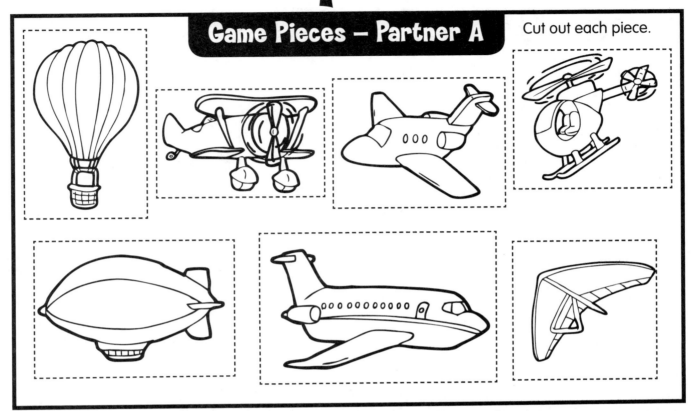

Game Pieces – Partner B

Cut out each piece.

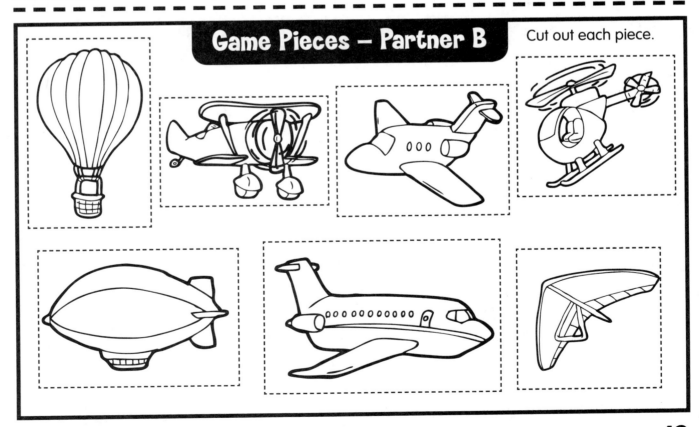

Alphabet Soup

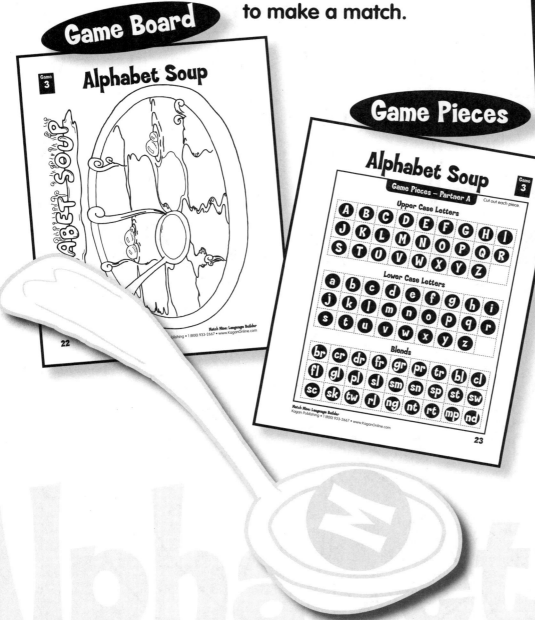

Partner A places letter or blend game pieces on the soup game board. Partner B cooperates with Partner A to make a match.

Game Board

Game Pieces

Vocabulary

- Aa
- Bb
- Cc
- Dd
- Ee
- Ff
- Gg
- Hh
- Ii
- Jj
- Kk
- Ll
- Mm
- Nn
- Oo
- Pp
- Qq
- Rr
- Ss
- Tt
- Uu
- Vv
- Ww
- Xx
- Yy
- Zz

- br
- cr
- dr
- fr
- gr
- pr
- tr
- bl
- cl
- fl
- gl
- pl
- sl
- sm
- sn
- sp
- st
- sw
- sc
- sk
- tw
- rl
- ng
- nt
- mp
- rt

Alphabet Soup

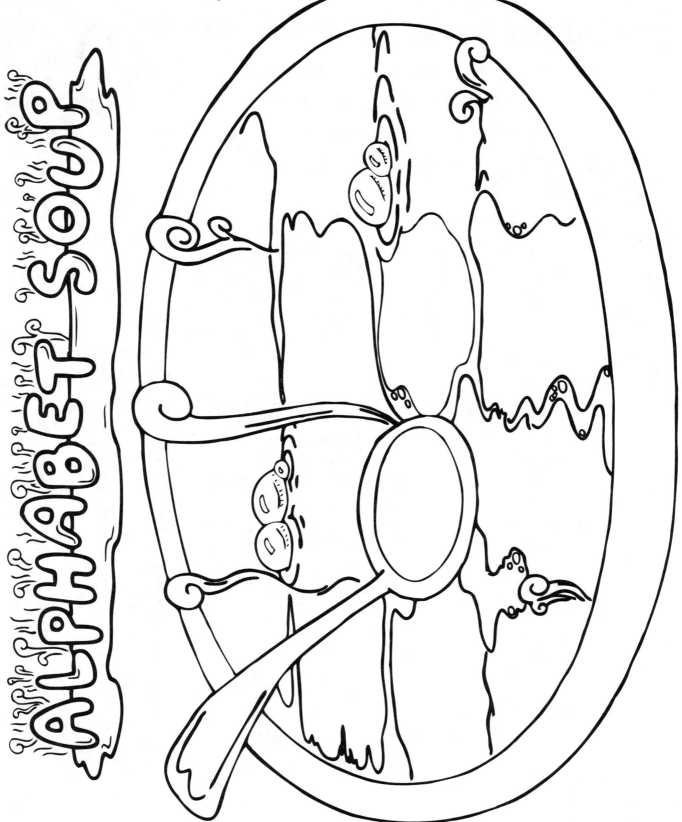

Match Mine: Language Builder
Kagan Publishing • 1 (800) 933-2667 • www.KaganOnline.com

Alphabet Soup

Game Pieces – Partner A
Cut out each piece.

Upper Case Letters

A B C D E F G H I
J K L M N O P Q R
S T U V W X Y Z

Lower Case Letters

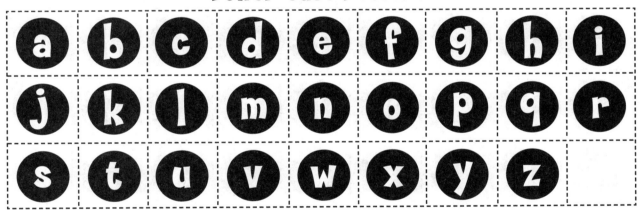

a b c d e f g h i
j k l m n o p q r
s t u v w x y z

Blends

br cr dr fr gr pr tr bl cl
fl gl pl sl sm sn sp st sw
sc sk tw rl ng nt rt mp nd

Alphabet Soup

Game Pieces – Partner B
Cut out each piece.

Upper Case Letters

A B C D E F G H I
J K L M N O P Q R
S T U V W X Y Z

Lower Case Letters

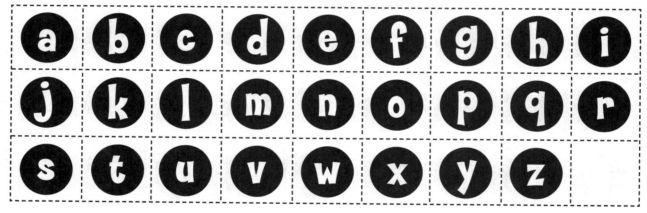

a b c d e f g h i
j k l m n o p q r
s t u v w x y z

Blends

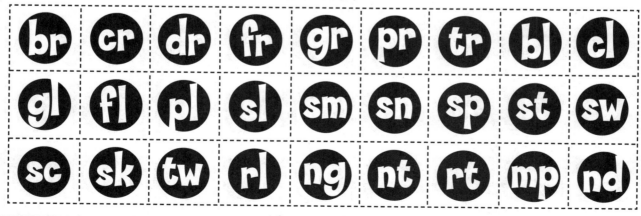

br cr dr fr gr pr tr bl cl
gl fl pl sl sm sn sp st sw
sc sk tw rl ng nt rt mp nd

Match Mine: Language Builder
Kagan Publishing • 1 (800) 933-2667 • www.KaganOnline.com

Around Town

Partner A places building game pieces on the town map game board. Partner B cooperates with Partner A to make a match.

Game Board

Around Town

Sunny St.

Ocean Blvd. Star Ave.

Fox Rd.

26

Game Pieces

Around Town

Game Pieces – Partner A

Cut out each piece.

27

Vocabulary

- Avenue
- Bank
- Boulevard
- Fire station
- Gas station
- Grocery store
- Intersection
- Movie theater
- Post office
- Restaurant
- Road
- School
- Store
- Street
- Town
- Toy store

Around Town

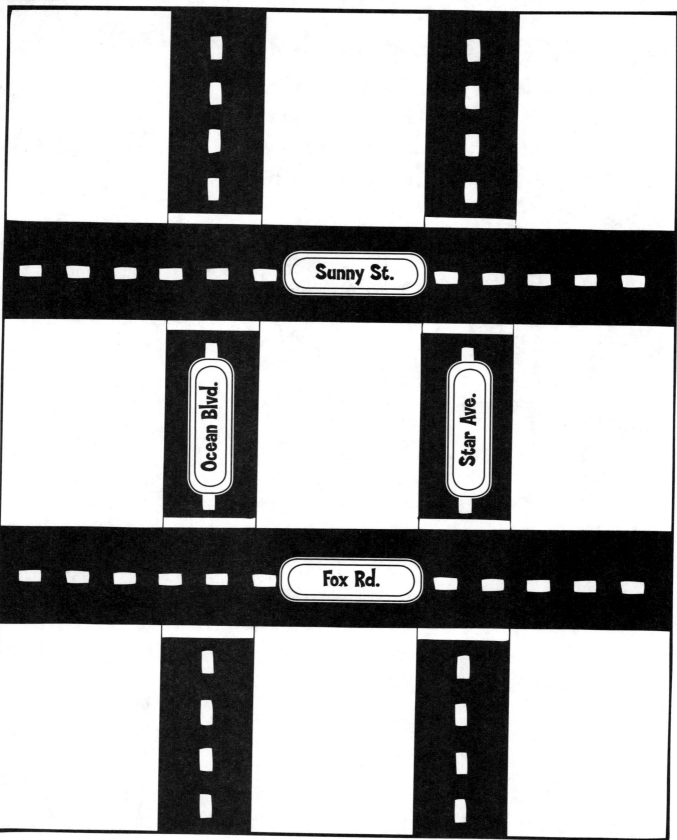

Sunny St.

Ocean Blvd.

Star Ave.

Fox Rd.

Around Town

Game Pieces – Partner A

Cut out each piece.

Around Town

Game Pieces – Partner B

Cut out each piece.

Match Mine: Language Builder
Kagan Publishing • 1 (800) 933-2667 • www.KaganOnline.com

Ball Sports

Partner A places ball game pieces on the storage shelf game board. Partner B cooperates with Partner A to make a match.

Game Board

Ball Sports

Game 5

30

Game Pieces

Ball Sports
Game Pieces – Partner A   Cut out each ball.

Game 5

31

Vocabulary

- Balls
- Baseball
- Basketball
- Bat
- Bowling ball
- Boxing gloves
- Football
- Golf ball
- Mask
- Snorkel
- Soccer ball
- Sports
- Tennis ball
- Tennis racquet
- Volleyball

Ball Sports

Ball Sports

Game Pieces – Partner A   Cut out each ball.

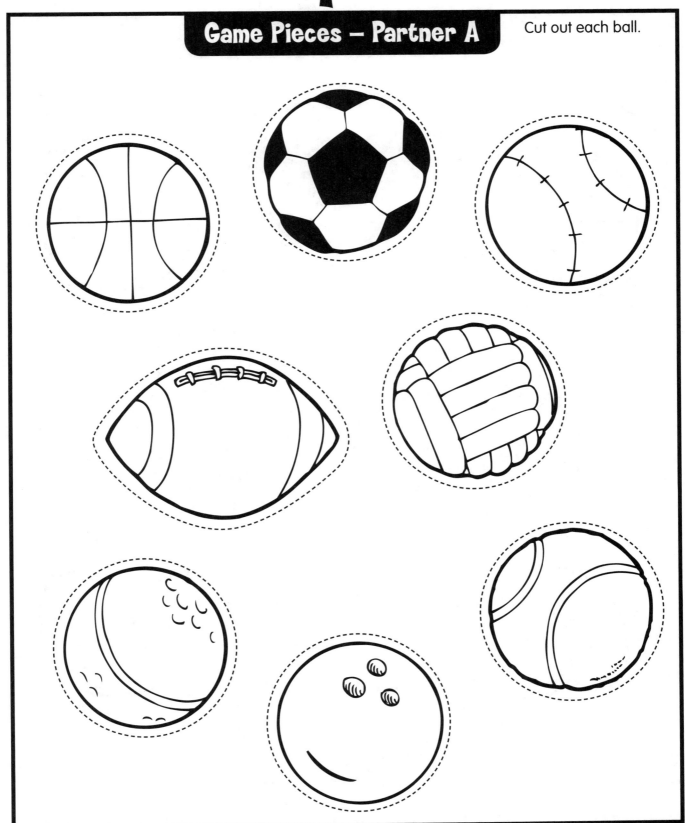

Ball Sports

Game Pieces – Partner B

Cut out each ball.

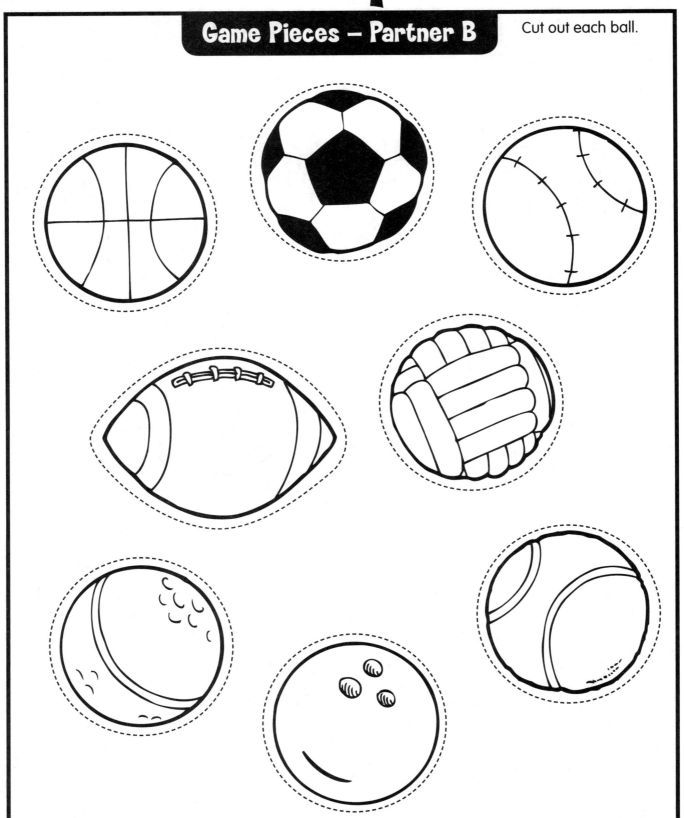

Match Mine: Language Builder
Kagan Publishing • 1 (800) 933-2667 • www.KaganOnline.com

Barnyard Animals

Partner A places animal game pieces
on the barnyard game board.
Partner B cooperates with Partner A
to make a match.

Vocabulary

- Animals
- Barn
- Barnyard
- Chicken
- Cow
- Door
- Duck
- Goat
- Goose
- Hen
- Horse
- Lamb
- Pig
- Sheep
- Turkey
- Window

Barnyard Animals

Match Mine: Language Builder
Kagan Publishing • 1 (800) 933-2667 • www.KaganOnline.com

Barnyard Animals

Game Pieces – Partner A
Cut out each animal.

Game Pieces – Partner B
Cut out each animal.

Bug's Life

Game 7

Partner A places bug game pieces on the outdoors game board. Partner B cooperates with Partner A to make a match.

Game Board

Game Pieces

Vocabulary

- Ant
- Bee
- Bee hive
- Beetle
- Bug
- Butterfly
- Caterpillar
- Cloud
- Dragonfly
- Fence
- Fish
- Flower
- Fly
- Grass
- Grasshopper
- Hills
- Insect
- Ladybug
- Leaves
- Plant
- Pond
- Rock
- Sky
- Tree

Bug's Life

Match Mine: Language Builder
Kagan Publishing • 1 (800) 933-2667 • www.KaganOnline.com

Bug's Life

Game Pieces – Partner A

Cut out each bug.

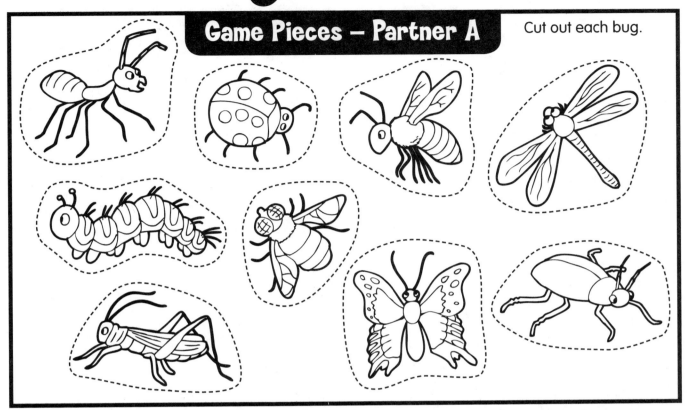

Game Pieces – Partner B

Cut out each bug.

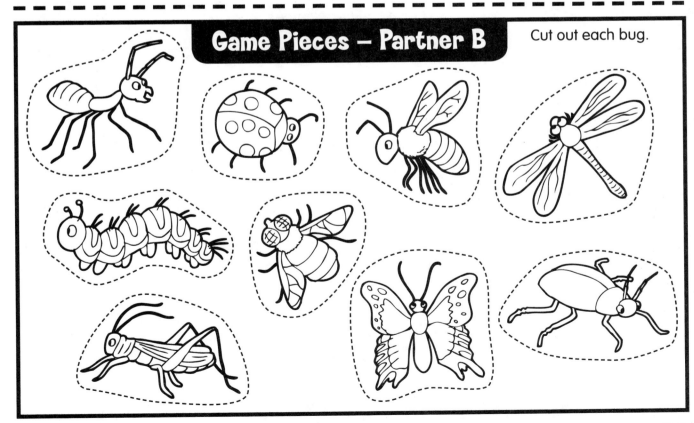

Circus Show

Partner A places circus game pieces on the big top game board. Partner B cooperates with Partner A to make a match.

Game Board

Circus Show

42

Game Pieces

Circus Show

Game Pieces – Partner A

Cut out each circus performer.

43

Vocabulary

- Big top
- Circus
- Clown
- Elephant
- Juggler
- Lion
- Lion tamer
- Magician
- Man
- Monkey
- Tent
- Tightrope
- Trapeze
- Unicycle
- Woman

Circus Show

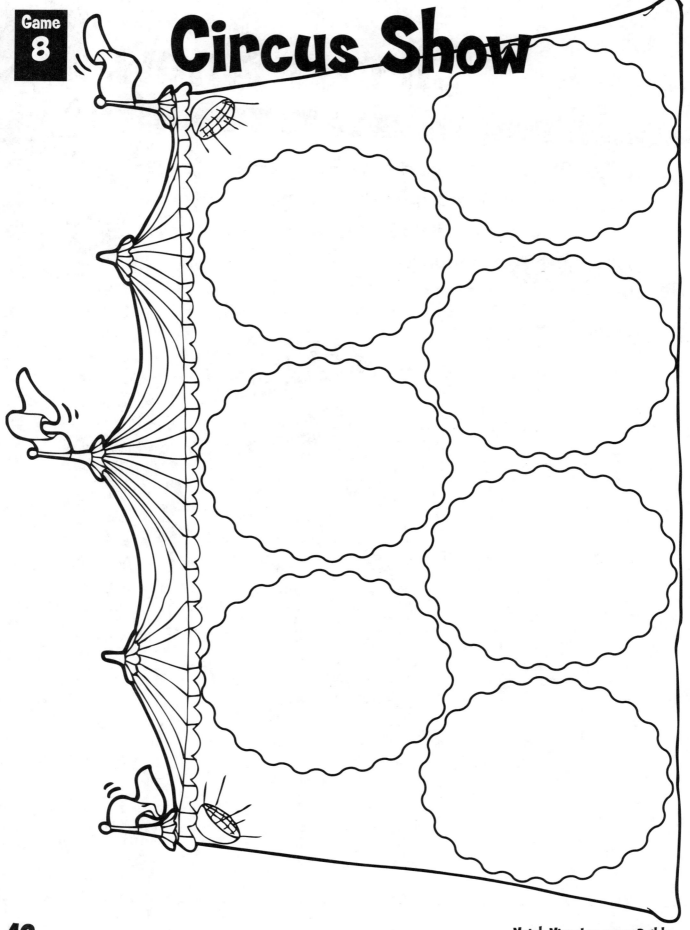

Match Mine: Language Builder
Kagan Publishing • 1 (800) 933-2667 • www.KaganOnline.com

Circus Show

Game Pieces – Partner A

Cut out each circus performer.

Circus Show

Game Pieces – Partner B   Cut out each circus performer.

Match Mine: Language Builder
Kagan Publishing • 1 (800) 933-2667 • www.KaganOnline.com

Coins in the Bank

Partner A places coin game pieces on the piggy bank game board. Partner B cooperates with Partner A to make a match.

Game Board

Game Pieces

Vocabulary

- Back
- Bottom
- Dime
- Front
- Left
- Middle
- Nickel
- Penny
- Piggy bank
- Quarter
- Right
- Top

Coins in the Bank

Match Mine: Language Builder
Kagan Publishing • 1 (800) 933-2667 • www.KaganOnline.com

Coins in the Bank

Game Pieces – Partner A

Cut out each coin.

Game Pieces – Partner B

Cut out each coin.

Fruit Basket

Partner A places fruit game pieces
on the fruit basket game board.
Partner B cooperates with Partner A
to make a match.

Game Board

Game Pieces

Vocabulary

- Apple
- Banana
- Basket
- Berry
- Blackberry
- Cherries
- Fruit
- Grapes
- Lemon
- Nectarine
- Orange
- Peach
- Pear
- Pineapple
- Plum
- Raspberry
- Strawberry
- Watermelon

Fruit Basket

Match Mine: Language Builder
Kagan Publishing • 1 (800) 933-2667 • www.KaganOnline.com

Fruit Basket

Cut out each fruit.

Game Pieces – Partner A

Fruit Basket

Cut out each fruit.

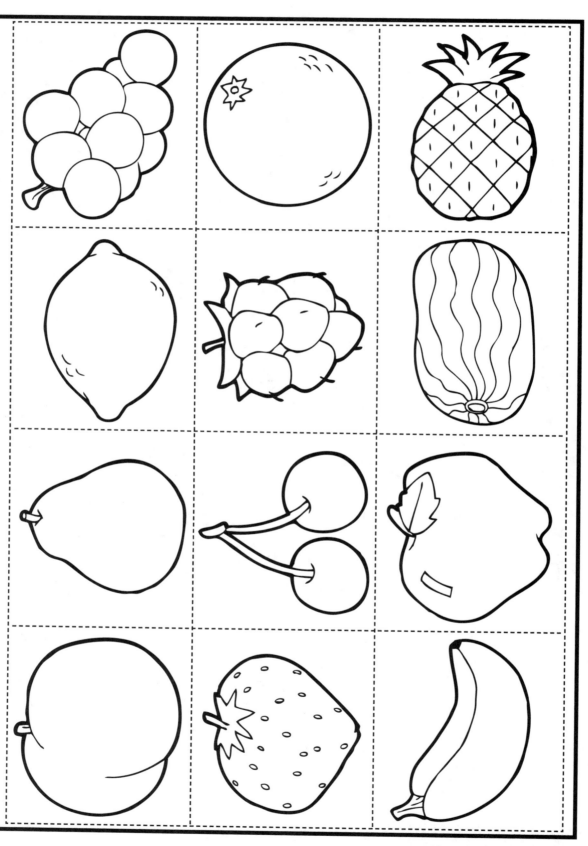

Match Mine: Language Builder
Kagan Publishing • 1 (800) 933-2667 • www.KaganOnline.com

Furniture

Partner A places furniture game pieces on the house floor plan game board. Partner B cooperates with Partner A to make a match.

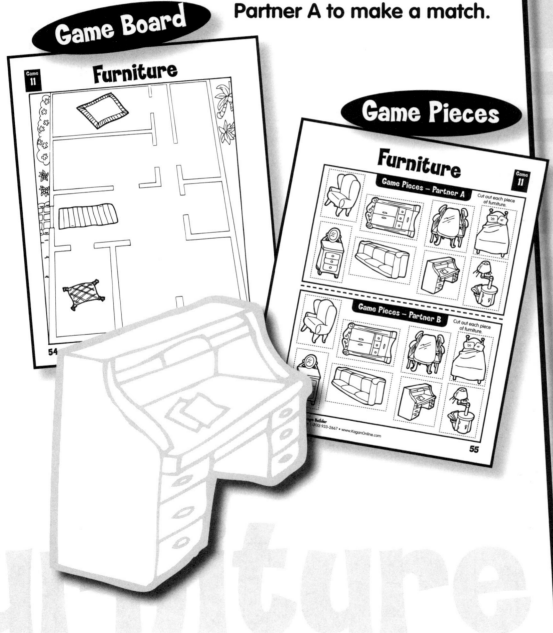

Game Board

Game Pieces

Vocabulary

- Armoire
- Bed
- Chair
- Chaise
- Couch
- Desk
- Dining table
- Drawers
- Dresser
- End table
- Lamp
- Magazine rack
- Mirror
- Pillows
- Room
- Rug
- Sofa
- Table
- Tassels

Furniture

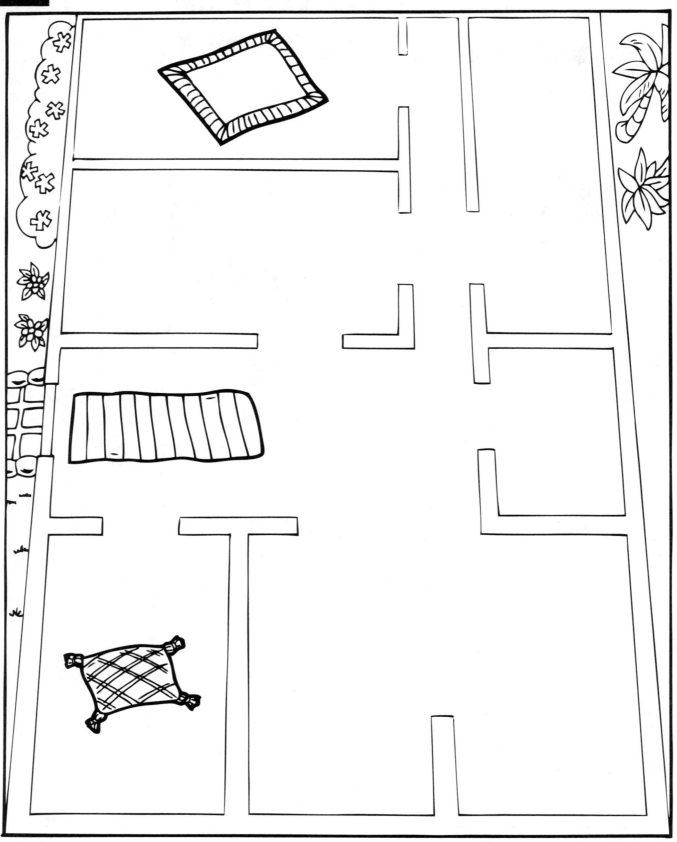

Match Mine: Language Builder
Kagan Publishing • 1 (800) 933-2667 • www.KaganOnline.com

Furniture

Game Pieces – Partner A

Cut out each piece of furniture.

Game Pieces – Partner B

Cut out each piece of furniture.

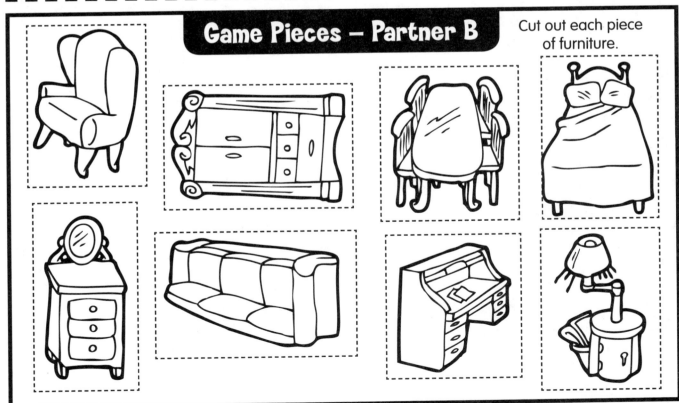

Home Appliances

Partner A places appliance game pieces on the house game board. Partner B cooperates with Partner A to make a match.

Game Board

Game Pieces

Vocabulary

- Appliance
- Computer
- Lamp
- Oven
- Refrigerator
- Telephone
- Television, TV
- Toaster
- Vacuum
- Washing machine

Home Appliances

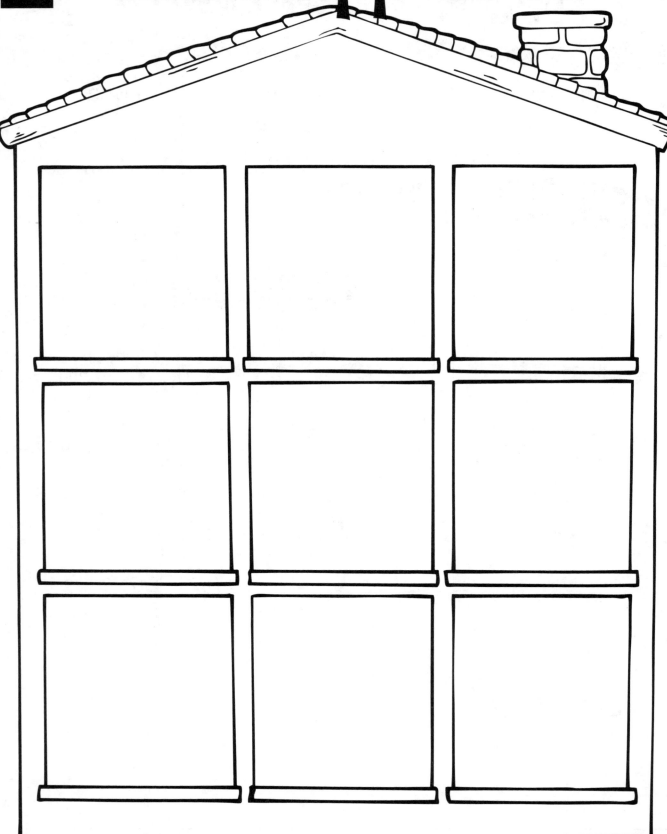

Match Mine: Language Builder
Kagan Publishing • 1 (800) 933-2667 • www.KaganOnline.com

Home Appliances

Game Pieces – Partner A

Cut out each appliance.

Home Appliances

Game Pieces – Partner B

Cut out each appliance.

Match Mine: Language Builder
Kagan Publishing • 1 (800) 933-2667 • www.KaganOnline.com

Human Body

Partner A numbers body parts on the human body game board. Partner B cooperates with Partner A to make a match.

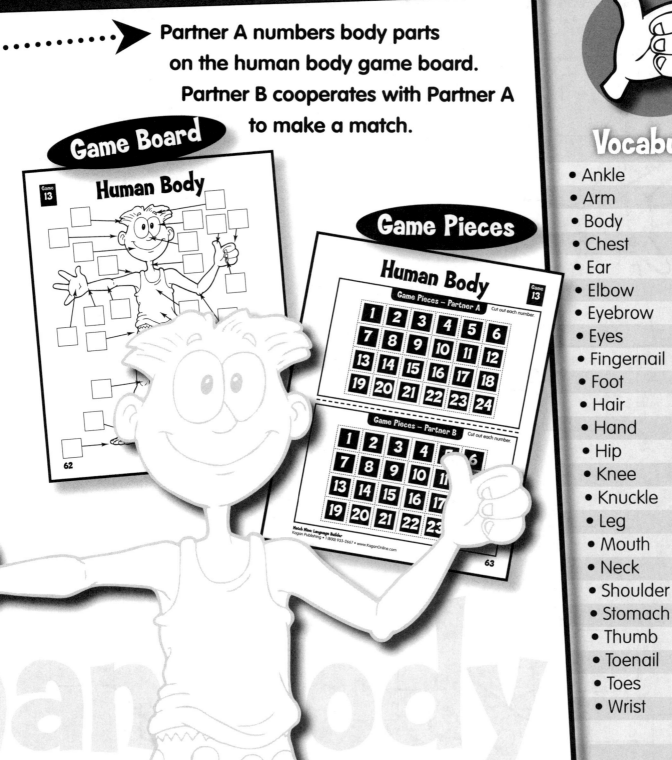

Game Board

Game Pieces

Vocabulary

- Ankle
- Arm
- Body
- Chest
- Ear
- Elbow
- Eyebrow
- Eyes
- Fingernail
- Foot
- Hair
- Hand
- Hip
- Knee
- Knuckle
- Leg
- Mouth
- Neck
- Shoulder
- Stomach
- Thumb
- Toenail
- Toes
- Wrist

Human Body

Match Mine: Language Builder
Kagan Publishing • 1 (800) 933-2667 • www.KaganOnline.com

Human Body

Game Pieces – Partner A

Cut out each number.

1	2	3	4	5	6
7	8	9	10	11	12
13	14	15	16	17	18
19	20	21	22	23	24

Game Pieces – Partner B

Cut out each number.

1	2	3	4	5	6
7	8	9	10	11	12
13	14	15	16	17	18
19	20	21	22	23	24

in the Closet

Partner A places clothes game pieces on the closet game board. Partner B cooperates with Partner A to make a match.

Game Board

in the Closet

Game Pieces

in the Closet

Vocabulary

- Belts
- Blankets
- Boots
- Cabinets
- Cats
- Closet
- Drawers
- Handles
- Hanger
- Hats, caps, visor
- Laundry basket
- Pants
- Pegs
- Pillow
- Rack
- Scarf
- Shirts
- Shoebox
- Shoes, slippers
- Skirts
- Socks
- Tee shirts
- Ties/bow tie
- Towels
- Umbrella

in the Closet

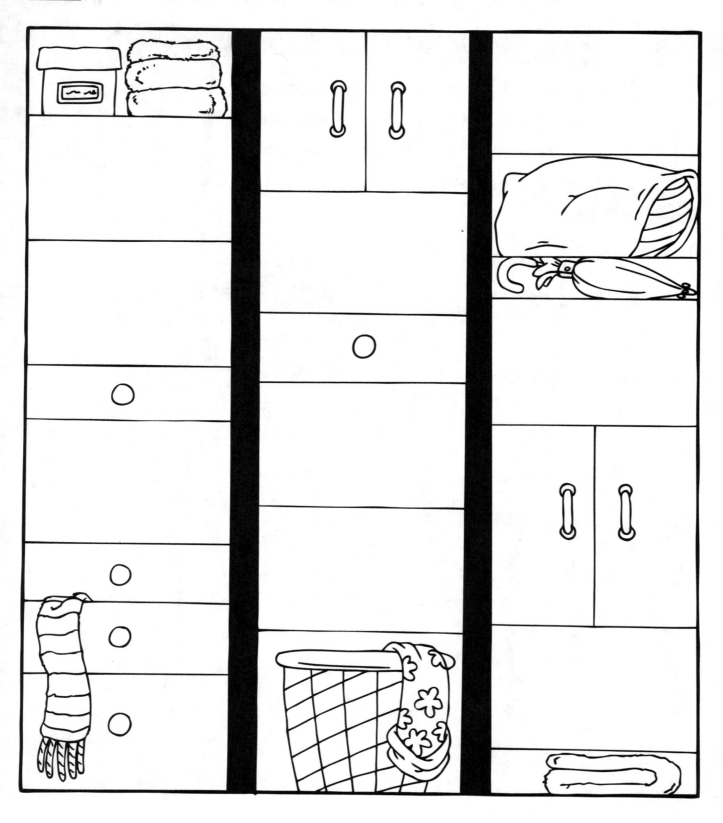

in the Closet

Game Pieces – Partner A
Cut out each piece.

Game Pieces – Partner B
Cut out each piece.

in the Refrigerator

Partner A places food game pieces on the refrigerator game board. Partner B cooperates with Partner A to make a match.

Game Board

Game Pieces

Vocabulary

- Bread
- Cake
- Celery
- Condiments
- Cookies
- Corn
- Desserts
- Door
- Drinks
- Eggs, carton
- Fish
- Fruit
- Grapes
- Juice
- Lettuce
- Meat
- Milk
- Mustard
- Pickles
- Pie
- Shelf
- Soda
- Steak
- Tortillas
- Vegetables
- Watermelon

in the Refrigerator

Game Pieces – Partner A

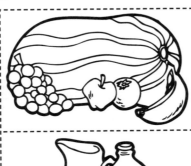

Cut out
each piece.

Game Pieces – Partner B

Cut out
each piece.

Jobs & Careers

> Partner A places career game pieces on the picture frame game board. Partner B cooperates with Partner A to make a match.

Game Board

Game Pieces

Vocabulary

- Barber
- Blow dryer
- Cash register
- Cashier
- Chef
- Cook
- Dentist
- Doctor
- Farmer
- Files
- Grocer
- Groceries
- Hairstylist
- Nurse
- Paint bucket
- Paint roller
- Painter
- Pilot
- Pipes
- Pitchfork
- Plumber
- Scissors
- Spatula
- Tooth

Jobs & Careers

Match Mine: Language Builder
Kagan Publishing • 1 (800) 933-2667 • www.KaganOnline.com

Jobs & Careers

Game Pieces – Partner A

Cut out each piece.

Jobs & Careers

Cut out each piece.

Making Sentences

Partner A builds sentences using the word game pieces on the sheet of paper game board. Partner B cooperates with Partner A to make a match.

Game Board

Making Sentences

Game 17 | Making Sentences

78

Match Mine: Language Builder
Kagan Publishing • 1 (800) 933-2667 • www.KaganOnline.com

Game Pieces

Making Sentences

Game 17

Game Pieces – Partner A   Cut out each word.

a	all	and	are	as	at	be	big	bird	blue
boy	but	buy	by	call	can	cat	come
dad	day	did	dinner	do	dog	eat	fast
for	food	from	fun	get	girl	give	go
good	had	happy	has	have	he	her
here	him	his	how	I	if	in	is	it	just
know	like	love	mad	make	man	me
mom	my	new	no	not	on	one	park
play	red	rose	...

happy

Vocabulary
• See vocabulary list on page 79.

the big blue bird

79

Making Sentences

Match Mine: Language Builder
Kagan Publishing • 1 (800) 933-2667 • www.KaganOnline.com

Making Sentences

a	all	and	are	as	at	be	big	bird	blue
boy	but	buy	by	call	can	cat	come		
dad	day	did	dinner	do	dog	eat	fast		
for	food	from	fun	get	girl	give	go		
good	had	happy	has	have	he	her			
here	him	his	how	I	if	in	is	it	just
know	like	love	mad	make	man	me			
mom	my	new	no	not	on	one	park		
play	red	rose	run	sad	she	sister			
slow	small	so	some	song	swing	the			
their	there	to	two	us	we	went	what		
were	when	will	with	would	you	zoo			

Making Sentences

a	all	and	are	as	at	be	big	bird	blue
boy	but	buy	by	call	can	cat	come
dad	day	did	dinner	do	dog	eat	fast
for	food	from	fun	get	girl	give	go
good	had	happy	has	have	he	her
here	him	his	how	I	if	in	is	it	just
know	like	love	mad	make	man	me
mom	my	new	no	not	on	one	park
play	red	rose	run	sad	she	sister
slow	small	so	some	song	swing	the
their	there	to	two	us	we	went	what
were	when	will	with	would	you	zoo

Match Mine: Language Builder
Kagan Publishing • 1 (800) 933-2667 • www.KaganOnline.com

Making Words

Partner A builds words using the letter game pieces on the sheet of paper game board. Partner B cooperates with Partner A to make a match.

a

Vocabulary

- a
- b
- c
- d
- e
- f
- g
- h
- i
- j
- k
- l
- m
- n
- o
- p
- q
- r
- s
- t
- u
- v
- w
- x
- y
- z

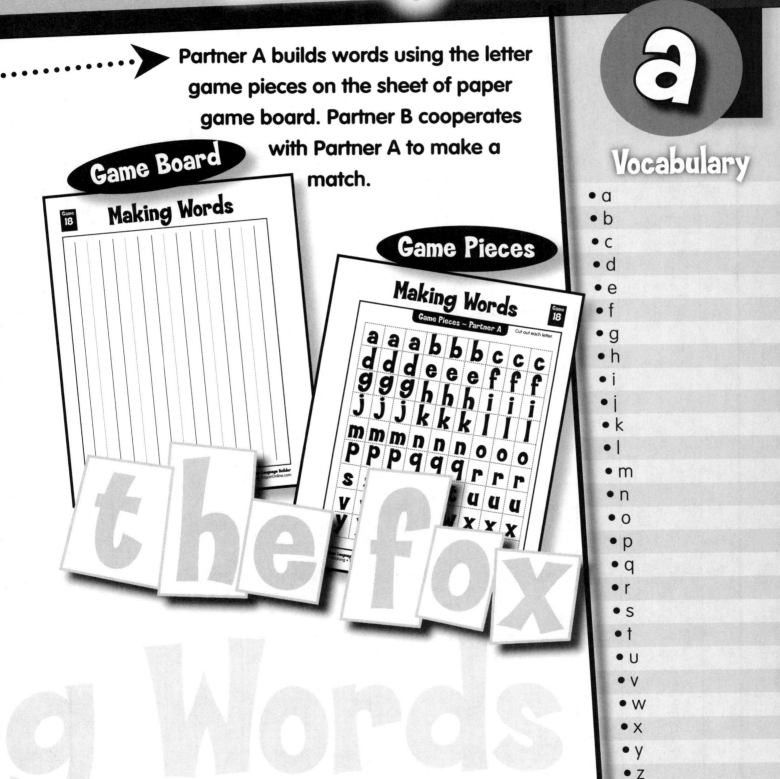

Game Board

Making Words

Game Pieces

Making Words

Game Pieces – Partner A   Cut out each letter.

a	a	a	b	b	b	c	c	c
d	d	d	e	e	f	f	f
g	g	g	h	h	h	i	i	i
j	j	j	k	k	k	l	l	l
m	m	m	n	n	n	o	o	o
P	P	P	q	q	q	r	r	r
s						u	u	u
v						x	x	x

Making Words

Match Mine: Language Builder
Kagan Publishing • 1 (800) 933-2667 • www.KaganOnline.com

Making Words

Game Pieces – Partner A

Cut out each letter.

a	a	a	b	b	b	c	c	c
d	d	d	e	e	e	f	f	f
g	g	g	h	h	h	i	i	i
j	j	j	k	k	k	l	l	l
m	m	m	n	n	n	o	o	o
p	p	p	q	q	q	r	r	r
s	s	s	t	t	t	u	u	u
v	v	v	w	w	w	x	x	x
y	y	y	z	z	z			

Making Words

Game Pieces – Partner B   Cut out each letter.

a	a	a	b	b	b	c	c	c
d	d	d	e	e	e	f	f	f
g	g	g	h	h	h	i	i	i
j	j	j	k	k	k	l	l	l
m	m	m	n	n	n	o	o	o
p	p	p	q	q	q	r	r	r
s	s	s	t	t	t	u	u	u
v	v	v	w	w	w	x	x	x
y	y	y	z	z	z			

Match Mine: Language Builder
Kagan Publishing • 1 (800) 933-2667 • www.KaganOnline.com

Olympic Sports

Partner A places Olympic sports game pieces on the medal game board. Partner B cooperates with Partner A to make a match.

Game Board

Game Pieces

Vocabulary

- Archery
- Bicycling
- Bow and arrow
- Boxing
- Cycling
- Diving
- Figure skating
- Gold
- Gymnastics
- Ice skating
- Man
- Medal
- Running
- Skiing
- Track and field
- Weightlifting
- Woman

Olympic Sports

Match Mine: Language Builder
Kagan Publishing • 1 (800) 933-2667 • www.KaganOnline.com

Olympic Sports

Game Pieces – Partner A

Cut out
each athlete.

Olympic Sports

Game Pieces – Partner B

Cut out
each athlete.

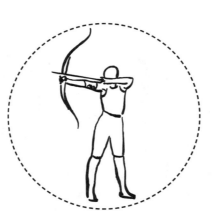

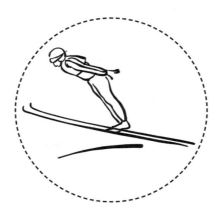

Match Mine: Language Builder
Kagan Publishing • 1 (800) 933-2667 • www.KaganOnline.com

Orchestra Music

Partner A places instrument game
pieces on the orchestra game board.
Partner B cooperates with Partner A
to make a match.

Game Board

Game Pieces

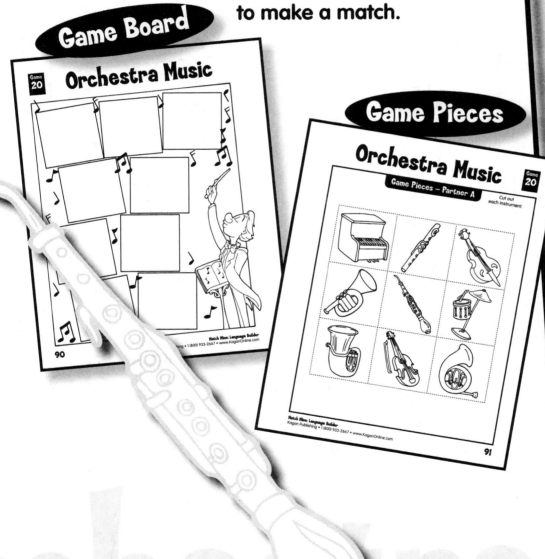

Vocabulary

- Cello
- Conductor
- Drums
- Flute
- French horn
- Instrument
- Oboe
- Orchestra
- Piano
- Trumpet
- Tuba
- Violin

Orchestra Music

Match Mine: Language Builder
Kagan Publishing • 1 (800) 933-2667 • www.KaganOnline.com

Orchestra Music

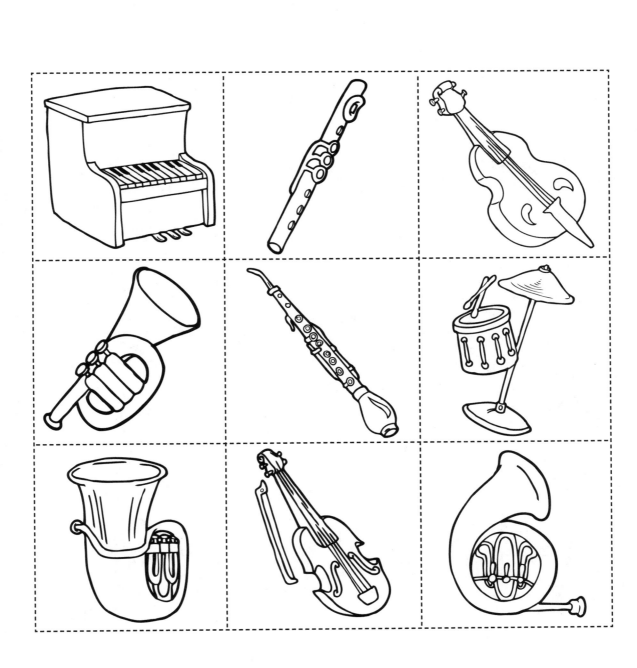

Game Pieces – Partner A

Cut out each instrument.

Orchestra Music

Game Pieces – Partner B

Cut out
each instrument.

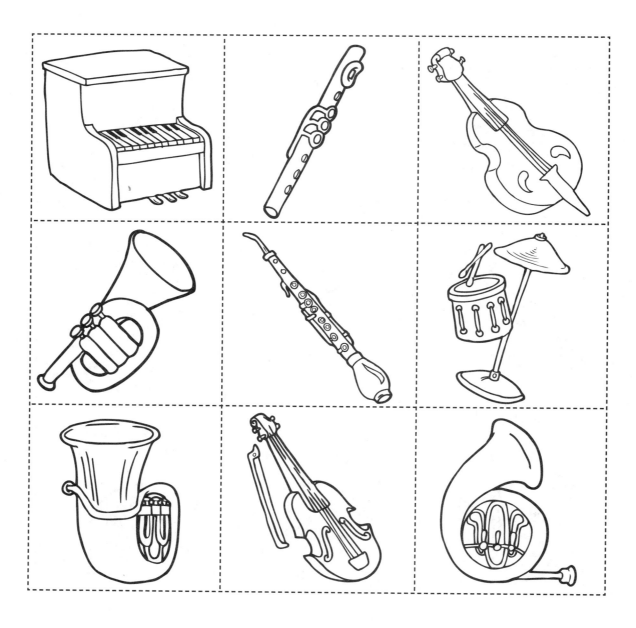

Match Mine: Language Builder
Kagan Publishing • 1 (800) 933-2667 • www.KaganOnline.com

Parking Lot

> Partner A places vehicle game pieces on the parking lot game board. Partner B cooperates with Partner A to make a match.

Game Board

Game Pieces

Vocabulary

- Bug
- Car
- Cruiser
- Limousine
- Motorcycle
- Parking lot
- Parking spot
- Race car
- Sports car
- Station wagon
- Street bike
- SUV
- Tree
- Truck
- Van

Parking Lot

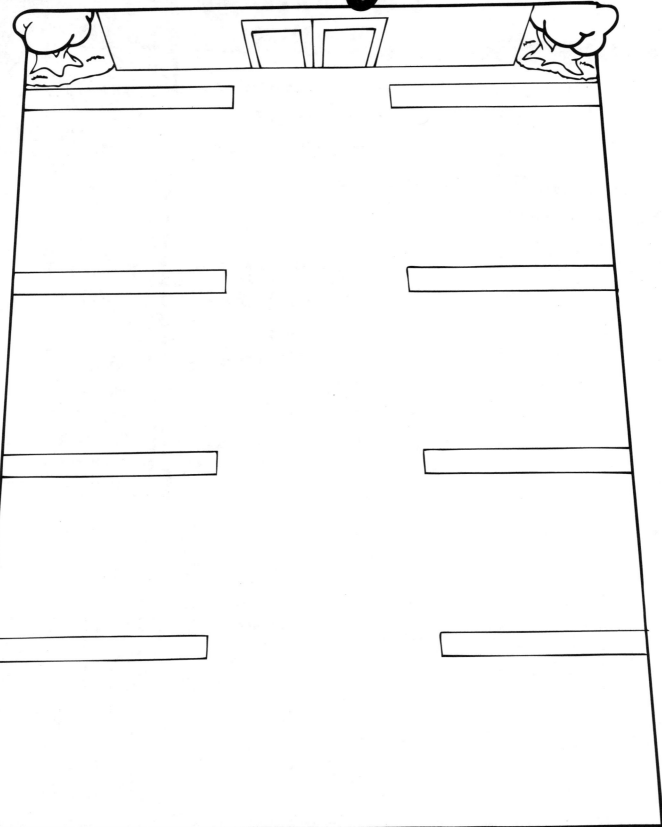

Match Mine: Language Builder
Kagan Publishing • 1 (800) 933-2667 • www.KaganOnline.com

Parking Lot

Game Pieces – Partner A

Cut out each vehicle.

Parking Lot

Game Pieces – Partner B
Cut out each vehicle.

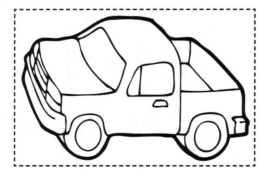

Match Mine: Language Builder
Kagan Publishing • 1 (800) 933-2667 • www.KaganOnline.com

Park Playground

Partner A places park game pieces on the park game board. Partner B cooperates with Partner A to make a match.

Game Board

Game Pieces

Vocabulary

- Bench
- Elephant
- Monkey bars
- Path
- Rings
- Sandbox
- Seesaw
- Slide
- Spring
- Swing set
- Swings
- Table
- Teeter-totter
- Tire swing
- Toy
- Tree

Park Playground

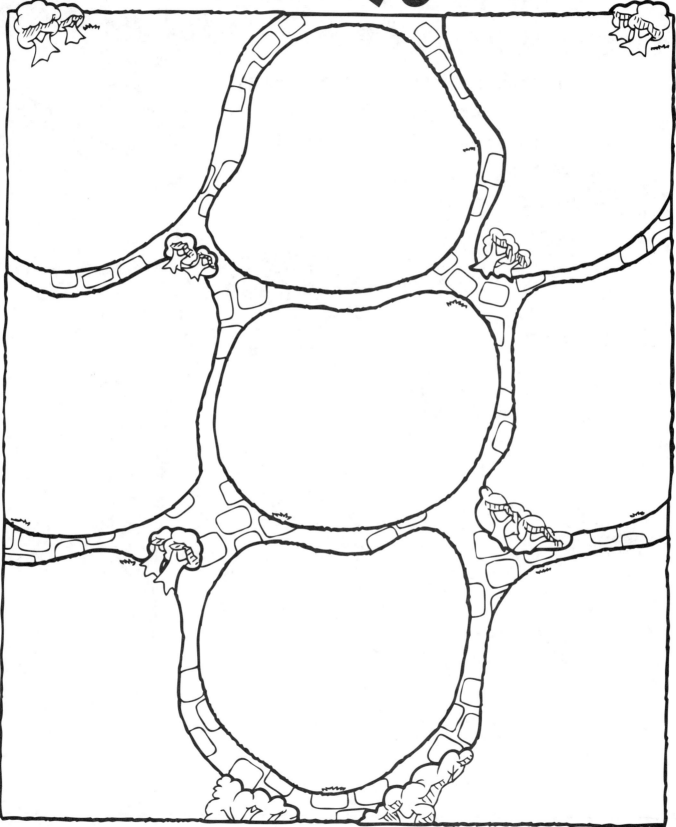

Match Mine: Language Builder
Kagan Publishing • 1 (800) 933-2667 • www.KaganOnline.com

Park Playground

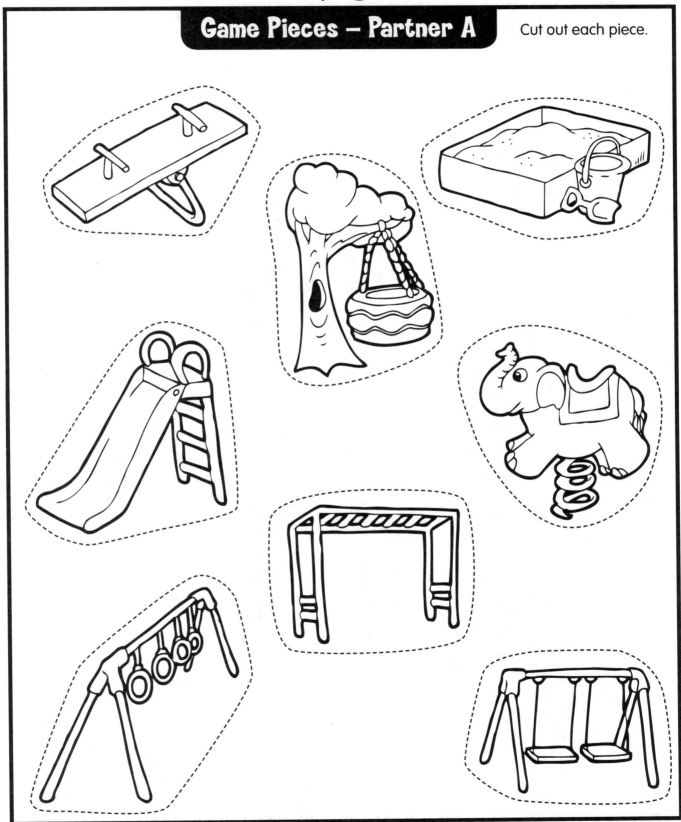

Game Pieces – Partner A　　Cut out each piece.

Park Playground

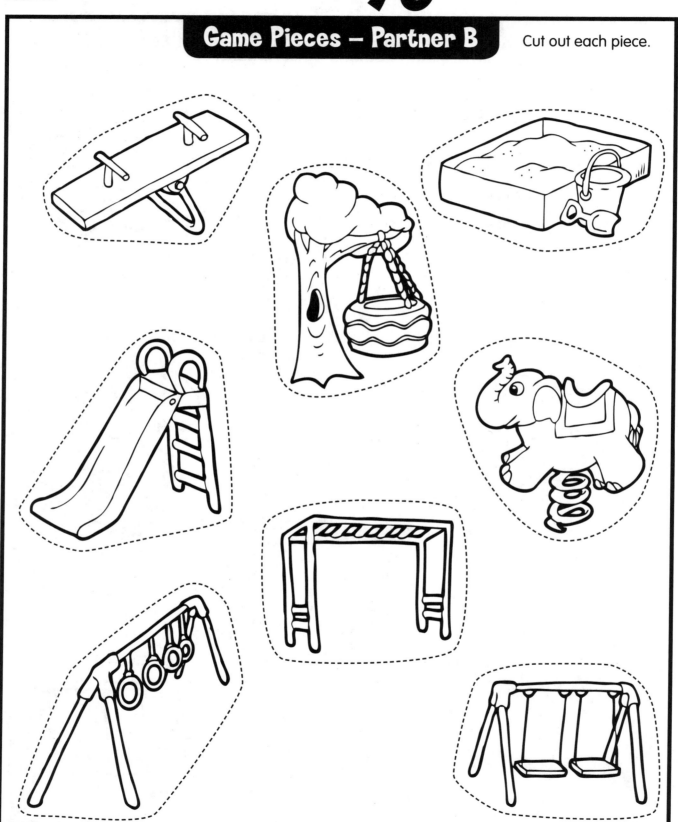

Partner A places pet game pieces on the pet store window game board. Partner B cooperates with Partner A to make a match.

Vocabulary

- Bird
- Cat
- Chameleon
- Dog
- Goldfish
- Hamster
- Pet
- Snake
- Turtle
- Window

Game Board

Game Pieces

Pet Store

Pet Store

Game Pieces – Partner A   Cut out each pet.

Pet Store

School Supplies

Partner A places school supply game pieces on the backpack game board. Partner B cooperates with Partner A to make a match.

Game Board

Game Pieces

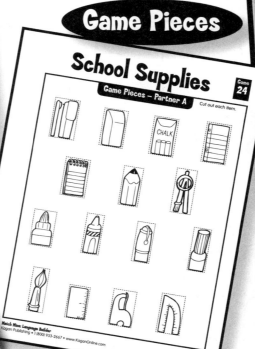

Vocabulary

- Backpack
- Brush
- Buckle
- Chalk
- Compass
- Crayon
- Eraser
- Glue
- Marker
- Notepad
- Paper
- Pen
- Pencil
- Pocket
- Pouch
- Protractor
- Ruler
- School supplies
- Scissors
- Stapler
- Strap
- Tape
- Zipper

School Supplies

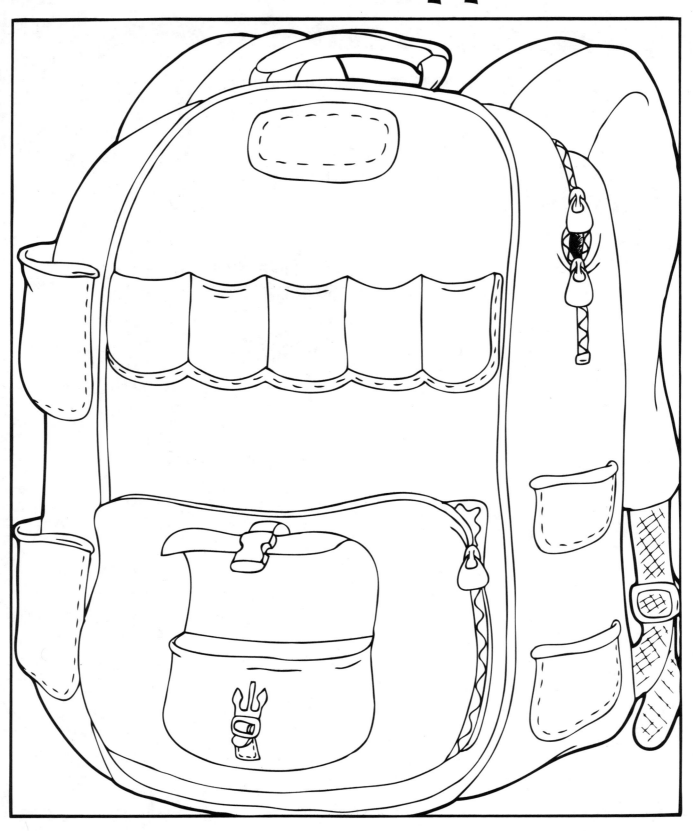

School Supplies

Game Pieces – Partner A

Cut out each item.

CHALK

School Supplies

Cut out each item.

CHALK

Match Mine: Language Builder
Kagan Publishing • 1 (800) 933-2667 • www.KaganOnline.com

Partner A places weather game pieces on the calendar game board. Partner B cooperates with Partner A to make a match.

Game Board

Game Pieces

Vocabulary

- Blowing
- Clouds
- Friday
- Lightning
- Monday
- Palm trees
- Partly sunny
- Rain drops
- Raining
- Saturday
- Snow
- Snowflakes
- Storm cloud
- Stormy
- Sun
- Sunday
- Sunny
- Sunshine
- Thursday
- Tuesday
- Wednesday
- Wind
- Windy

Today's Weather

How's the Weather Today?

Sunday

Monday

Tuesday

Wednesday

Thursday

Friday

Saturday

Match Mine: Language Builder
Kagan Publishing • 1 (800) 933-2667 • www.KaganOnline.com

Today's Weather

Game Pieces – Partner A

Cut out each piece.

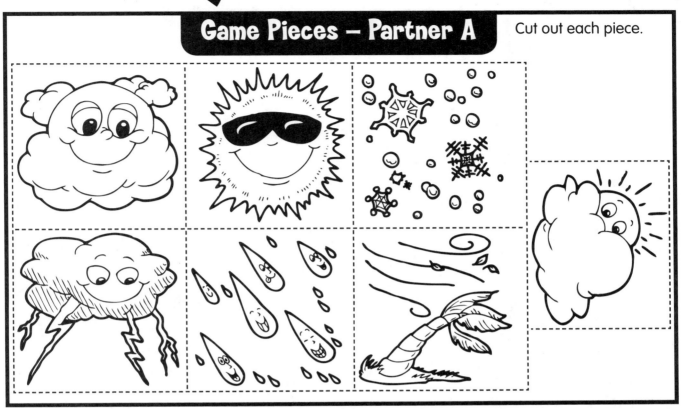

Game Pieces – Partner B

Cut out each piece.

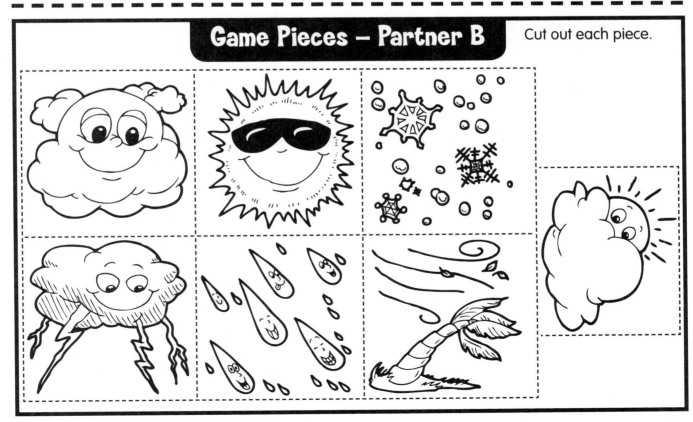

Partner A places tool game pieces on the pegboard game board. Partner B cooperates with Partner A to make a match.

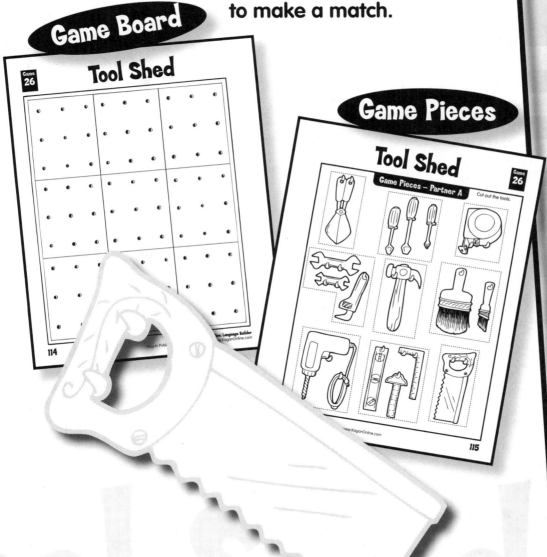

Game Board

Game Pieces

Vocabulary

- Clippers
- Drill
- Hammer
- Level
- Paint brushes
- Saw
- Screwdrivers
- Shears
- Square
- Tape measure
- T-Square
- Wrenches

Tool Shed

Match Mine: Language Builder
Kagan Publishing • 1 (800) 933-2667 • www.KaganOnline.com

Tool Shed

Game Pieces – Partner A

Cut out the tools.

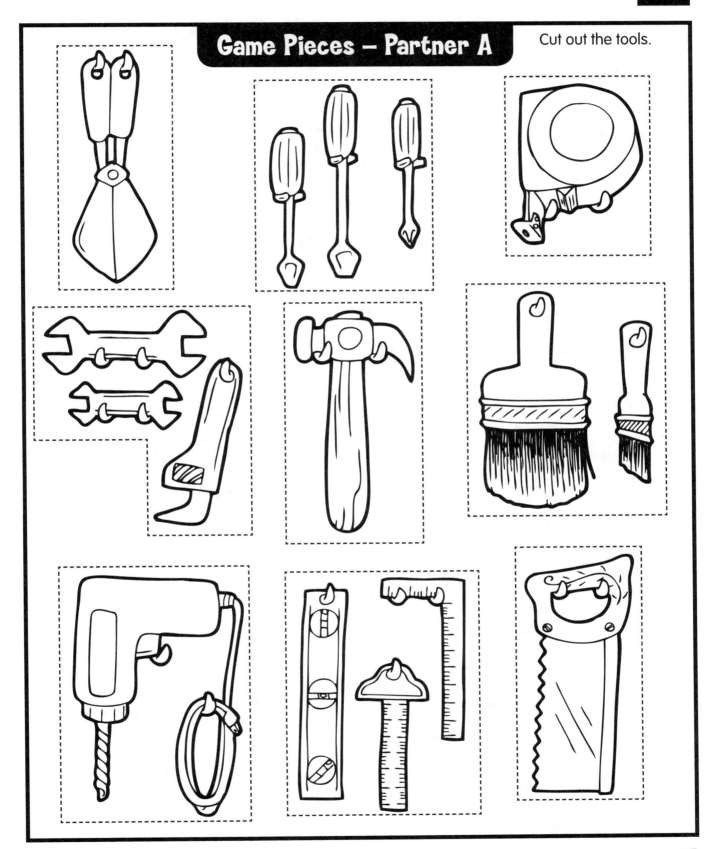

Tool Shed

Game Pieces – Partner B

Cut out the tools.

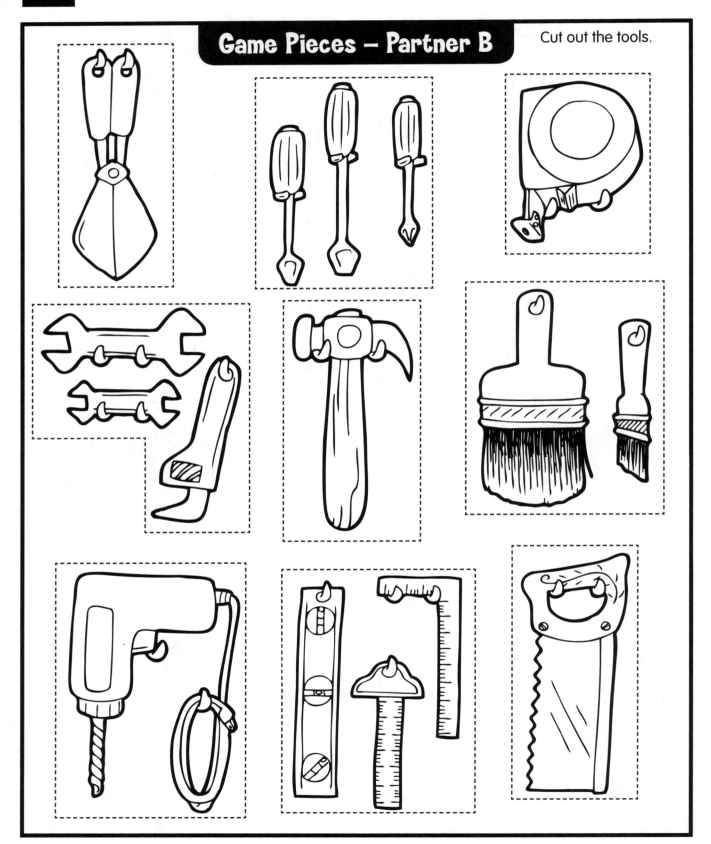

Match Mine: Language Builder
Kagan Publishing • 1 (800) 933-2667 • www.KaganOnline.com

Vegetable Garden

Partner A places vegetable game pieces on the garden game board. Partner B cooperates with Partner A to make a match.

Game Board

Game Pieces

Vocabulary

- Bell pepper
- Broccoli
- Carrot
- Cauliflower
- Corn
- Garden
- Lettuce
- Onion
- Packet
- Peas
- Row
- Seeds
- Squash
- Stick
- Vegetable
- Zucchini

Vegetable Garden

Match Mine: Language Builder
Kagan Publishing • 1 (800) 933-2667 • www.KaganOnline.com

Vegetable Garden

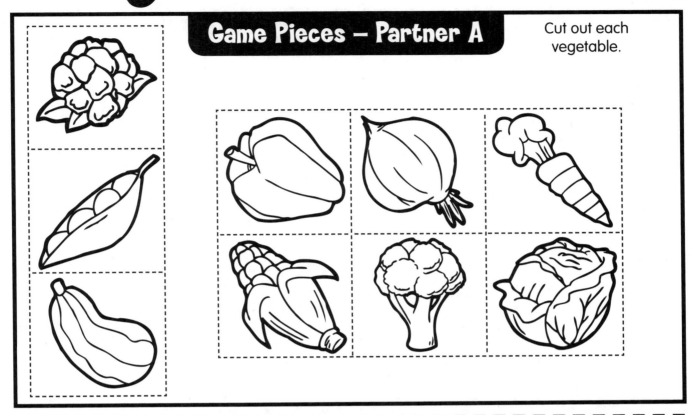

Game Pieces – Partner A

Cut out each vegetable.

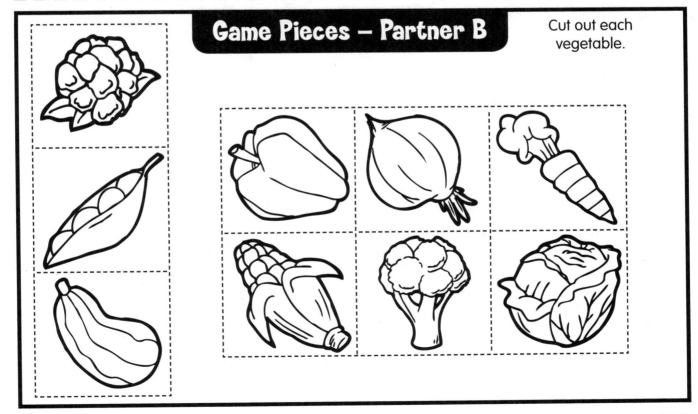

Game Pieces – Partner B

Cut out each vegetable.

Water Transport

Partner A places water transportation game pieces on the ocean game board. Partner B cooperates with Partner A to make a match.

Game Board

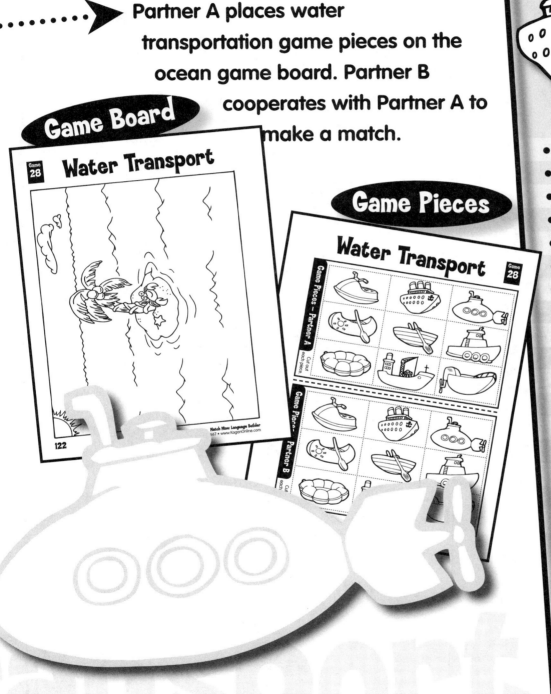

Game Pieces

Vocabulary

- Anchor
- Canoe
- Clouds
- Crab
- Cruise ship
- Island
- Jet Ski
- Motor
- Motor boat
- Oars
- Oil Tanker
- Palm Tree
- Raft
- Row boat
- Sailboat
- Sails
- Sea star, starfish
- Submarine
- Sun
- Tanker
- Tires
- Tugboat
- Water
- Wave runner

Water Transport

Water Transport

Game Pieces – Partner A

Cut out each piece.

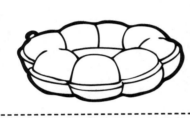

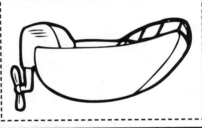

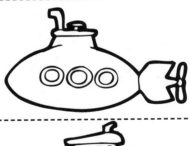

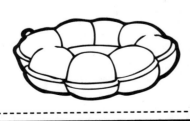

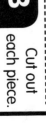

Game Pieces – Partner B

Cut out each piece.

Work Vehicles

Partner A places work vehicle game pieces on a road game board. Partner B cooperates with Partner A to make a match.

Game Board

Game Pieces

Vocabulary

- 18 Wheeler
- Ambulance
- Big rig
- Car carrier
- Dump truck
- Fire truck
- Ice cream truck
- Left turn
- Police car
- Right turn
- Road
- Straight
- Street
- Tow truck
- Tractor
- Tractor trailer
- Tree
- Turn

Work Vehicles

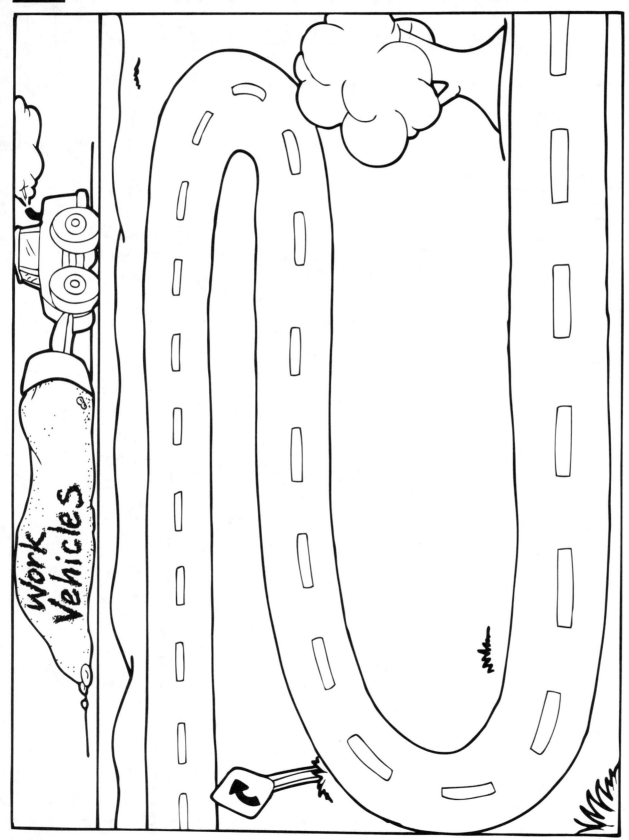

Work Vehicles

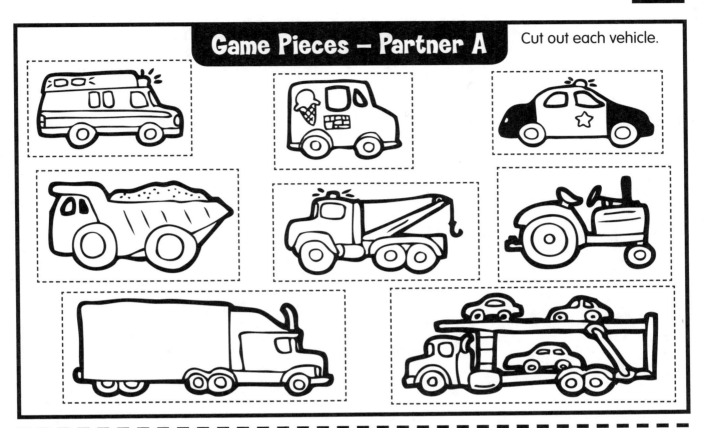

Game Pieces – Partner A   Cut out each vehicle.

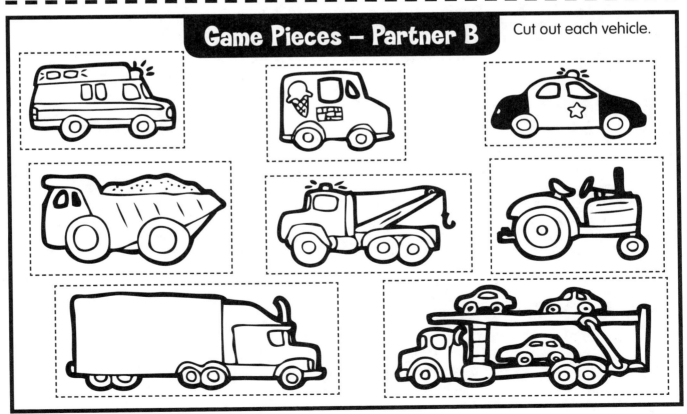

Game Pieces – Partner B   Cut out each vehicle.

Zoo Animals

Partner A places zoo animal game pieces on the zoo game board. Partner B cooperates with Partner A to make a match.

Game Board

Game 30

Zoo Animals

THE ZOO

130

Game Pieces

Zoo Animals

Game 30

Game Pieces – Partner A Cut out each animal.

Cut out each animal.

131

Vocabulary

- Bushes
- Ducks
- Elephant
- Entrance
- Fence
- Giraffe
- Kangaroo
- Lake
- Lion
- Monkey
- Path
- Rocks
- Shrubs
- Tree
- Zebra

Zoo Animals

Match Mine: Language Builder
Kagan Publishing • 1 (800) 933-2667 • www.KaganOnline.com

Zoo Animals

Game Pieces – Partner A
Cut out each animal.

Game Pieces – Partner B
Cut out each animal.

Match Mine: Language Builder
Kagan Publishing • 1 (800) 933-2667 • www.KaganOnline.com

Notes

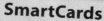